STEPPING WESTWARD

First published in paperback format by Coverstory books, 2020

ISBN 978-1-9162899-1-8

Copyright © Berta Lawrence, Christopher Lawrence, John Allen, Tom Furniss, Peter Haggett 2020

The right of Berta Lawrence to be identified as the author of this work has been asserted in accordance with the Copyright, Designs and Patents Act 1988.

Cover image: "Megalith 2, Stanton Drew" © Adrian Lewis and reproduced with the gracious approval of the photographer.

All rights reserved.

No part of this publication may be reproduced, circulated, stored in a system from which it can be retrieved, or transmitted in any form without the prior permission in writing of the publisher.

www.coverstorybooks.com

BERTA LAWRENCE

STEPPING WESTWARD

Selected Poems

Collected and transcribed
by Christopher Lawrence

Introduced by John Allen,
Tom Furniss and Peter Haggett

Edited by Tom Furniss

Other Books by Berta Lawrence

Escape from Danger: Tales of the West Country from 1497 to 1685, illustrated by E.M. Dawson (E.J. Arnold & Son, 1948).

The Tiler's Apprentice and Other Stories, illustrations by A. Crabtree (E.J. Arnold & Son, 1948).

Fun and Frolic Stories, with pictures by Frank Jennens (Bruce Publishing Co., 1948).

The Stickleback (U.T.B., 1948).

A Somerset Journal (Westaway Books, 1951).

Quantock Country (Westaway Books, 1952), reissued as a facsimile edition by the Library Service of Somerset County Council in 1989.

The Bond of Green Withy (Werner Laurie, 1954), reissued by Country Book Club (1956), Cedric Chivers of Bath (1973) and Somerset Books (1997).

The Nightingale in the Branches (Laurie, 1955).

Coleridge and Wordsworth in Somerset (David and Charles, Newton Abbot, 1970).

Somerset Legends (David & Charles, Newton Abbot, 1973).

Discovering the Quantocks (Shire Publications, Aylesbury, 1974).

Exmoor Villages, A-Z (Exmoor Press, Dulverton, 1984).

A Somerset Voice (Chew Magna, 2016).

Contents

Berta Lawrence: Life and Writings 7
Editing the Poems 13

I: COASTAL EXMOOR

Exit from Cleeve 21
The Cloister Garden, Dunster 22
Culbone 23
At Ash Farm 24
Harriet at Lynmouth, 1812 25

II: EXMOOR PLACES

Exmoor Geometry 29
Stone Circle 30
Exmoor Tale Teller 31
An Exmoor Thorn 32
Exmoor Mistletoe 33

III: EXMOOR PEOPLE

Nativity, Exmoor 37
Ladies in Snowdrop Valley 38
Barbellion on Exmoor 39
Names of Exmoor Girls 40

IV: THE BRENDONS

Naked Boy: A Standing Stone 43
Deserted Village 44
At Leigh Barton 45
Treborough Man 46

V: THE QUANTOCKS

Alfoxton 49
A Man at the Window: A Sonnet for STC 50
Bicknoller: In Memory of Richard Jefferies 51
Moorland Ponies 52

VI: SEDGEMOOR

Sedgemoor Catalogue (From a High Window) 55
Night on Sedgemoor 56
Cadbury 57

VII: MELANCHOLY

The Old Pond 61
Meadow Close 62
A Christmas Child 63
Haworth Postman 64
The Wind and the Dark 65

VIII: MEMORIES

Moon Daisies: A Sonnet 69
Boulevard Fleuri..70
Nightingales of the Auvergne 71
Pebble from a Barrow 72
Man in the Moon...73
Charles's Wain 74

IX: THE FOUR SEASONS

Seasons...77
Yellow Spring 78
April Garden...79
Swallows 80
June Scents..81
Midsummer...82
Lazy Summer..83
Summer's End 84
Apples...85
Red Feast 86
Jack Frost...87
Season of Sleep 88
Blackthorn Winter...89

X: NATURE, FIELDS AND FLOWERS

Field Map...93
The Green Wheatfield 94
The Old Paddock 95
Old Lane 96
Daffodils...97
Four Winds 98
Wild Geese 99
Reflections...100
Roadside Garden 101

Acknowledgements..103

Berta Lawrence: Life and Writings[1]

The aim of this collection of Berta Lawrence's poetry is to make it more readily available to a wide readership and to support our claim that she deserves to be recognised as one of the major Somerset literary figures of the twentieth century.[2] Best known for her novels and topographic and historical books about Somerset, including a pioneering book about the impact of the Quantocks on Coleridge and the Wordsworths in 1797-98, she shifted readily between literary forms, producing children's stories, scholarly works, regional novels, essays for journals, poetry, even lyrics for music. Her books about Somerset and her novels can still be obtained via the Internet, but her poems – more than fifty of which were originally published in *Children's Education* and the *Exmoor Review* – are not so well known or easily available. Yet it is in her poetry – sometimes complex and haunting, sometimes apparently naïve – that her most subtle responses to Somerset's landscapes, legends and people can be heard.

Annie Bertha Buckingham was born on 17th May 1906, the youngest of three daughters of a Buckinghamshire farmer in the parish of North Marston in the Vale of Aylesbury. She showed a love of literature and began writing stories and poems at an early age. Academically gifted, she gained a place at Aylesbury Grammar School in 1917 and was the first girl in the school to win a County Major Scholarship to university in 1924. She read English Literature and French at Reading University (then a college of the University of London), graduating with First Class Honours in 1927 and going on to gain a Diploma in Education. One of her first teaching posts was in France, where she was appointed as a teaching Assistant at the University of Clermont Ferrand in the Auvergne province of the Massif Central. This involved lecturing in

---

[1]. This account is based on John Allen and Peter Haggett's Introduction to *A Somerset Voice: The Poetry of Berta Lawrence* (Chew Magna, 2016), adapted, rewritten and edited by Tom Furniss.

[2] Critical appreciation of Berta Lawrence's work has thus far been less than it deserves. See Victor Bonham-Carter *Exmoor Writers and Their Works*, vol. I (The Exmoor Press, 1987), Victor Bonham-Carter, 'Berta Lawrence: An Appreciation', *Exmoor Magazine*, Winter 2003, vol.25, 36-37, and James Crowden, *Literary Somerset* (Flagon Press, Chard, 2010), p. 111. Also see https://www.exmoor-nationalpark.gov.uk/Whats-Special/culture/literary-links/berta-lawrence,

English Language and Literature to French undergraduates and teaching English in French schools in the local area. It was at one of these schools that she met John Frederick ('Jack') Lawrence, then aged 23, who was also teaching there. Jack was born in Halifax in 1907 and educated at Halifax Grammar School and Durham University, where he read History with Honours. Berta and Jack married in the summer of 1932 and moved to the village of Wembdon just to the west of Bridgwater in Somerset, where they lived for the rest of their long lives. Jack – a writer in his own right – taught History for nearly forty years at Dr Morgan's School, one of the county's oldest and most well-regarded schools, retiring as Deputy Head in 1970. Berta taught French at the Girls' Grammar School in Bridgwater and English at the French Convent in Langport, bussing there each day across the (sometimes flooded) Somerset Levels.[3]

Wembdon was the base from where Lawrence explored and wrote about Somerset for the next seventy years. Her locales ranged from the nearby Quantocks, through the Sedgemoor marshes in the centre of the county, to the rugged Exmoor hill country in the west (Fig. 1).

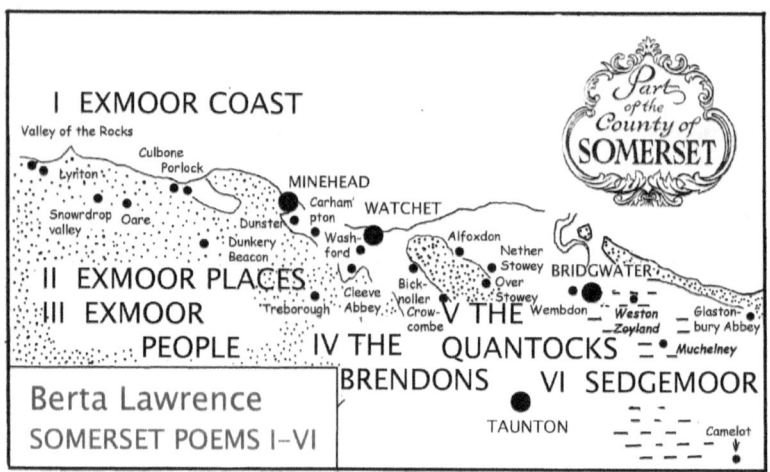

[3] See John Allen and Peter Haggett, 'Berta and Jack Lawrence: A West Country Literary Partnership Remembered', *Exmoor Review*, 2005, vol. 46, pp. 58-59.

Figure 1. A map of 'Parts of the County of Somerset' from Berta Lawrence's *A Somerset Journal* (Westaway Books, 1951, pages 104-5) drawn by Frederick Brown. Locations of places featured in her poems, where they can be traced, have been added. Stipple indicates hill country and horizontal dashes the marshes of Sedgemoor.

She showed a similar sweep in time, writing poems on its earliest inhabitants right through to essays on contemporary rural craftsmen. She demonstrated a remarkable power to conjure up the spirit of these much-loved landscapes, their changing seasonal moods, their notable visitors.

Writing for Children

While her two children were still small, Lawrence began to write stories and poems for the journal *Child Education*, which published over one hundred of her works over the next two decades. During the 1940s she wrote short stories and scripts for the BBC, notably for the iconic 'Children's Hour' radio programme. After the war, she gathered some of her children's stories together in four illustrated books: *Escape from Danger: Tales of the West Country from 1497 to 1685* (1948), *The Tiler's Apprentice and Other Stories* (1948), *Fun and Frolic Stories* (1948), and *The Stickleback* (1948).

Books on Somerset's Topography and Local History

Lawrence is perhaps most well known for her topographical and historical books on Somerset. The twelve chapters of *A Somerset Journal* (1951) reflect the changing Somerset year in all its variety. Topics range from the Parrett osier beds in the east to the heights of Exmoor in the west. It has, as one critic put it, 'the air and voice of the West Country on every page'. Thirty years later, Victor Bonham Carter in his *Exmoor Writers* (1987) suggested it deserved to be reprinted as it stood. *Quantock Country* (1952) has a beguilingly simple structure: an opening chapter on the hills, two chapters on the villages, and a final chapter on 'a few Quantock people'. Her scholarly study, *Coleridge and Wordsworth in Somerset* (1970), tells the fascinating story of that poetic 'annus mirabilis' of July 1797 to July 1798 when the Quantocks were the crucible in which Samuel Taylor Coleridge, William Wordsworth and Dorothy Wordsworth revolutionised English poetry. Lawrence skilfully weaves their poems and prose into the lanes of Nether Stowey, the combes of Holford, and the rock-strewn beach at Kilve. *Somerset Legends* (1973) reveals a further dimension to her deep knowledge of the county. In chapters on 'Saints', 'Rogues', 'Kings' and would-be Kings, she explores the rich tapestry of Somerset legends and the collective memory of the landscape. She continued to research and celebrate the area in *Discovering the Quantocks* (1974) and *Exmoor Villages* (1984).

Somerset Novels

Lawrence's fascination with Somerset's landscape and history was also expressed in a pair of regional novels. *The Bond of Green Withy* (1954) describes family struggles in the flat, water-logged, willow-growing area of Sedgemoor. The action takes place over the period 1890-1917 and concerns the struggles of Catherine England and her husband to build up a withy-grower's business for their sons. The narrative is dominated by the challenges posed by the special wetland environment of this part of the county. Frieda, the central character of *The Nightingale in the Branches* (1955), lives on a farm in one of the long, branching combes on the eastern side of the Quantock hills and is studying in the Upper Sixth Form of a Girls' Grammar School in a nearby town. The plot takes place over a single year at the end of World War II and explores Frieda's relations with her father, friends and staff in the school, and her growing sense of romance, but the strongest parts are the puzzles set by the changing Quantock farming year and the 'genius loci' of the landscape. Despite their success, Berta did not write any more novels. We'll therefore never know if she would have done for central Somerset what R.D. Blackmore did for Exmoor.

Articles and Essays

Lawrence published occasional essays throughout her writing life, but her output increased remarkably after the publication of *Somerset Legends* in 1973. Her historical and topographical essays about the West Country appeared in serials such as *Chambers Journal*, *The Guardian*, *The Countryman*, *The Lady*, *Western Morning News*, *South West Catholic History*, *Somerset and West* and *Dorset Life*. She also wrote essays on the West Country Coleridge circle – Humphrey Davy, Robert Southey and John Chubb – for the journals of the Charles Lamb Society and the Thomas Hardy Society.

Poetry

Lawrence wrote poetry for more than eighty years. *The Great Orchestra and Other Poems*, containing twenty early poems, was published by her parents when she was fifteen. On her 97th birthday (17 May 2003) she wrote her last poem, 'The Roadside Garden', for a friend who had come to visit. In between, she published thirty-eight poems in *Children's Education* and seventeen in the *Exmoor Review*. After her death in 2003, her son Christopher Lawrence found among her papers over two hundred poems, many of which were unfamiliar to him. Some were completed, some in handwritten drafts, only a few apparently published. Christopher kept a file of these poems and typed up those still in handwriting. After Christopher's untimely death in April 2015, John Stuckey found amongst his papers the box file containing the typed poems. Unfortunately, the poems could not be found on his computer, so John Allen and Peter Haggett undertook the task of retyping them. They then privately published *A Somerset Voice* (Chew Magna, 2016), containing sixty poems and a memoir of Lawrence's life and work. This pamphlet was circulated among family and friends and lodged in local and county libraries and in the five repository libraries where national collections of scholarly work are kept. The full transcript of all 220 known poems was lodged at the Somerset Record Office.

The fifty-nine poems in the present volume are those originally chosen for inclusion in *A Somerset Voice*. They exhibit a variety of styles, forms and topics. Those written for *Child Education* are often in four-line rhyming stanzas and are dominated by natural observations: the changing year, seasonal festivals, flowers and hedgerows, migrating birds, changing night skies. The high regard in which they were held is indicated by the fact that the musicologist William Hughes Parry chose one of them – 'Four Winds' – to set to music in 1973. In later poems written for mature readers she experimented with more ambitious and complex forms (including free verse, subtle rhyme patterns, and the sonnet). Two aspects of their structure stand out. The first is that even in poems describing the present, she often reminds the reader of the past. A good example is 'The Nightingales of the Auvergne', in which two present-day lovers listen to the same nightingale's song which was heard by Roman soldiers marching on their way to battle and by French resistance prisoners in a Nazi interrogation centre facing execution or transportation. (In this respect, it recalls Keats's 'Ode to a Nightingale'.) A second trait is the role of the final line or stanza. Having led us quietly in one direction, they often spring a surprising turn which jolts us into renewed attention and re-reading.

John Allen, Tom Furniss, Peter Haggett

Editing the Poems

What an audacious undertaking – to edit, and even revise, the poems of a writer who was an accomplished author and published poet who is no longer around to accept or reject proposed changes. It began as a reflex action, with no thought of preparing the poems for publication. Peter Haggett sent me a copy of *A Somerset Voice* because I had expressed an interest – as a family friend, a recently retired university lecturer in English, co-author of a student textbook on poetry, and published poet – in reading the poems. I was immediately struck by their subtle, haunting quality but troubled by not infrequent errors in punctuation, typos, rhythm, lineation and phrasing. As I read and re-read, I made 'corrections' with a pencil, as if I were preparing to discuss possible revisions with the author. In doing this I was almost automatically following a habit developed over nearly forty years of responding to the written work of students and the drafts of professional colleagues. Perhaps I felt able to do this because the poems were in a privately printed pamphlet rather than a published book that had gone through a professional editorial process. I was also emboldened by the account of their provenance in the introduction to *A Somerset Voice*. Many of the poems were discovered in handwritten form and as early drafts and had not therefore undergone the fine-tuning necessary for publication. They were typed out and then typed again, with the potential for errors to creep in at each stage. Even those poems that had been published were copied from versions found in Lawrence's papers rather than from the journals they had appeared in, thus missing out any last-minute revisions that might have been made during the publication process. John Allen and Peter Haggett admitted in *A Somerset Voice* that they were not expert judges of poetry, and Peter confessed to me in an email that his retyping of the poems was not always attentive to finer points of punctuation or lineation.

Despite these superficial faults, I began to feel that the poems were good enough to be published in book form, with some editing and gentle revision. I wrote to Peter Haggett with a tentative proposal along these lines and he forwarded it to Lawrence's family. They responded enthusiastically to the idea and so Peter sent the Word document of *A Somerset Voice* to me, which greatly facilitating the process of revising the poems and material from the memoir.

Editing and revising the poems went through several stages, beginning with those pencilled revisions made on the paper version of *A Somerset Voice*. The amount of revision has differed with each poem, sometimes merely involving light re-punctuation, the correction of typos, or the introduction of line breaks or stanza divisions. But some poems seemed to call for more intrusive revision, involving adjustments to rhythm, metre and even vocabulary. In every case, though, the object was to enable the poems to embody what I took to be the poet's original intentions. I will illustrate the process by looking at a couple of poems that underwent more revision than most. Having loved, studied and taught Coleridge's poetry for several decades and written my own poems about Coleridge, I was especially intrigued by 'A Man at the Window'. This is the version in *A Somerset Voice*:

A Man at the Window

Through this small window he had smelt the sweet
Summer breath of the lime-flowers, and the reek
Of the tan-pits; Wednesday every week
Had watched the carrier rumble up the street
To fetch his letters; children running by
Carrying the Quantock foxgloves in July,
Gipsies with whortleberries from the combes,
And broom-squires crying heather-headed brooms;
And last, in carts for Christmas market, all the store
Of holly from Alfoxden woods jolt past his door.
This February midnight Lime Street roofs shine bright
With diamond dust of frost: walls, empty road, blanched white
By the round white moon. Outside his window lies
The enchanter's world, the conjured paradise.
How the cold moonlight glitters in his eyes!

My initial pencil revisions concentrated on moments of what seemed like awkward rhythm and under-achieved imagery – deleting 'had' in line 1 and the definite articles in lines 2, 3 and 6, inserting 'tree' into 'lime-tree flowers' in line 2 (to create an allusion to Coleridge's 'This Lime-Tree Bower my Prison'), deleting 'the sweet' in line 1 (a too-obvious and unnecessary adjective), and putting a squiggly line under 'round white' in line 13 (two adjectives that add very little to our mental image of the moon, one of them merely repeating 'white' at the end of the previous line). But then I realised that this poem is a sonnet (with an extra line at the end). The standard form of the sonnet genre is 14 lines in iambic pentameter (five beats, 10 syllables) with a rhyme scheme that corresponds with divisions into octave (first eight lines) and sestet (last six lines) or into three quatrains (four-line groups) and a concluding couplet. Most of the lines in 'Man at the Window' contain five beats and some – such as the first – are in iambic pentameter. There is also a complex, if somewhat unusual rhyme scheme: abbaccddeeffggg. Recognising this poem as a sonnet entailed rethinking my revisions, cancelling some and introducing others. Although 'sweet' at the end of line 1 does not greatly enhance our sense of the smell of the lime flowers, for example, it is necessary for the rhyme with 'street' and so earns its place. The new task was to help the poem adhere better to the sonnet form, mostly through metrical revisions. The final version is as follows:

A Man at the Window: A Sonnet for STC

Through this small window he had smelt the sweet
Summer breath of the lime-flowers, and the reek
Of nearby tan-pits; Wednesday every week
Had watched the carrier rumble up the street
To fetch his letters; children running by
Carrying the Quantock foxgloves in July,
Gipsies with whortleberries from the combes,
And broom-squires crying heather-headed brooms;
And carts for Christmas market with the store
Of holly from Alfoxden woods jolt past his door.
This February midnight Lime Street roofs shine bright
With diamond dust of frost and walls blanched white
By silent moon. Outside his window lies
The enchanter's world, the conjured paradise.

How the cold moonlight glitters in his eyes!

The insertion of 'nearby' in line 3 turns a four-beat line into an iambic pentameter line (the tan-pits really were nearby Coleridge's cottage); lines 9 and 12 had to be cut down from 6 beats to 5 beats (line 12 was especially awkward rhythmically); I wrestled at length with line 10 – 'Of holly from Alfoxten woods jolt past his door' – because it too has 6 beats, but I gave up in the end because it's a great line in which every word counts; I still didn't think 'round white' added anything to 'moon' and so substituted 'silent' – which introduces an allusion to Coleridge's 'Frost at Midnight'. The last line is set off by a space, which is sometimes done with sonnets with an extra line. And a subtitle was added to highlight that this is a sonnet and that it's about Coleridge (Coleridge often used his initials – STC – when referring to himself). This poem, then, underwent several minor revisions, but they were all made to help it become a better sonnet.

I have included all fifty-nine poems that Allen and Haggett chose for *A Somerset Voice*, made some changes to the order of the groups of poems they created, changed some of the names of the groups, and redistributed some poems into different groups. The brief introductions to the groups are modified versions of those that appear in *A Somerset Voice*. The only poem that doesn't seem to fit into any of the groups is one of Lawrence's best and most characteristic poems. I therefore insert it here and explain the revisions it has undergone:

The Stone Lover

Man is the lover of stone.
The staggering child picks up pebbles on the beach.
The boy throws stones to bring down conkers.
From the core of a stone
Ancient man made a tool,
With a flake of flint
Sharpened his killing arrow;
He worshipped a stone,
Vast, alone and phallus shaped.
With stone Man built huts ranged in circles
Or clustered, like beehives;
To remember a battle he raised a cairn.
Built castles, bridges, gateways of stone,
Cathedrals, prisons, cowsheds with stout pillars;

Set up stone slabs graved with names of the dead.
Built city-walls and sea walls to face the tide,
Garden-walls to support the espaliered pear.

Grey limestone, speckled granite
Found on the moors,
Red sandstone, blue lias
Found on the coast; blue stone
From mountains,
Quarried and shaped.

Those who lifted the Stonehenge sarsens
Had played with pebbles on the beach,
Thrown stones at the wild crab-apples.

In addition to correcting typos and modifying punctuation, I made the following changes: 'Infant man' in line 5 became 'Ancient man'; 'From' in line 6 became 'With'; a long, rhythmically awkward line – 'He worshipped a stone, vast, solitary, and phallus-shaped' – became 'He worshipped a stone / Vast, alone and phallus shaped' ('alone' is better rhythmically and creates an internal rhyme with 'stone' – other poems suggest that Lawrence was fond of internal rhymes); two later lines – 'With stone he built castles, bridges, gateways, / Cathedrals and prisons, and cowsheds with stout pillars' – were modified to improve rhythm and to eliminate 'With stone he', which seemed redundant because it's already said a couple of lines earlier ('With stone Man'); line breaks in the second section were rearranged; 'from the moors' and 'from the coast' became 'Found on the moors' and 'Found on the coast' for the rhythm and for parallelism; in the line 'These lie quarried and shaped' the first two words seemed redundant; the last three lines were formed into a new section to mark the shift in thought; 'Man who lifted' became 'Those who lifted'.

I hope readers – especially those in Berta Lawrence's family – feel that the relatively extensive revisions to these two poems have not distorted but helped to foreground their intrinsic qualities. I have attempted to revise all the poems as lightly and tactfully as possible. I believe that Lawrence would have undertaken similar revisions herself if she had prepared them for publication in book form and would have welcomed an editor's suggestions. As we have seen, she was a published writer with a BA Honours degree in English and French. The language of her published books – I have only read *Coleridge and Wordsworth in Somerset* and *The Bond of Green Withy* – demonstrates a high level of technical proficiency. Allen and Haggett tell us that her love of writing poetry was not an uncritical one. She dismissed her early work as 'immature', and many of her later poems were written and rewritten, fashioned and refashioned. In her absence, that is what I have tried to do.

Tom Furniss

I: COASTAL EXMOOR

From Watchet west to Porlock lies a strip of land, rarely more than a mile wide, between the Severn Sea (the Bristol Channel) and the hill country of the Brendons and Exmoor. In this sequence of poems, we move west along this coast, starting with 'Exit from Cleeve' which describes the closing of the Cistercian monastery there in 1537 by Henry VIII and the pensioning-off of its monks. 'The Cloister Garden, Dunster' is set three miles further along the coast. The next two poems are based in the parish of Culbone near Porlock where the medieval church is evoked. 'At Ash Farm' imaginatively recreates the incident in 1797 when Coleridge, according to his own account, dreamed his great poem 'Kubla Khan' and started to write it out, only to be interrupted by 'a person from Porlock'. Four miles to the west lies Lynmouth across the county border in Devon. 'Harriet at Lynmouth, 1812' is set in the summer of 1812 when the poet Shelley (then aged 20) and his wife Harriet (17) spent part of their honeymoon there. Harriet later committed suicide by drowning and Shelley was drowned off Leghorn in Italy.

Exit from Cleeve

Early morning smelling of new-mown grass,
In silence they pass through the gatehouse,
Thirty men in white homespun,
Heads bowed and hands in sleeves.

The gatehouse is inscribed
'Closed to no honest man'.
But to them it is closed forever.
One last look towards the cloister
Then for the last time they cross the garth,
Stand in the lane and hear once more
The shallow prattle of the Roadwater
Running down their Vallis Florida
Between the buttercups and mallows.
Never again will they climb the narrow stair
To eat beneath bent angel-heads
Sweetly smiling between their carven curls,
Never again tread that chill tiled floor
Blazoned with arms of Charlemagne and Lion Heart.
Now they stand in the stony Washford lane,
Eyes turned towards the Brendon Hills
And on their flocks at pasture.

The Cloister Garden, Dunster

Here the black-gowned Benedictines walked,
Released from church and cell;
Sat on a bench and talked,
Enjoying a spell of sunshine and ease,
Watching the bees,
Lured by the spicy smell
Of lovage and thyme in the herb-plot,
Hearing the overhead rush of wings
As pigeons flew home to the dovecot.

Here sit the tourists, weary,
Writing coloured postcards to tell
Of visits to castle and yarn-market.
They drop pennies in the Wishing Well,
Watch bees humming round the lavender,
Butterflies sunning on the bergamot.
A few years ago they too could have seen
The pigeons fly home to the dovecot.[4]

---

[4] 'The medieval dovecot at Dunster has now been closed because of vandalism' (Berta Lawrence).

Culbone

Welsh saint Beuno climbed
The zigzag path from Porlock
Between oak-woods and the sea,
Raised his cell-church of wattle
Among trees and streams.
The bearded charcoal-burners
Sent up smoke between the oaks,
And in a lonely clearing
The outcast lepers lived
Cut off by the stream.
Poets walked here: talkative Coleridge,
Taciturn Wordsworth, wild-eyed Dorothy,
With Hazlitt the Shropshire lad,
And rustic Chester from Stowey.
Byron's daughter built her house,
Stately, Italianate,
Not a stone of it left,
Yet a little church stands
Among trees and streams.

At Ash Farm

A late November day,
A fox's rank scent lay
On sodden yellow leaves
Fallen in Ash Farm lane
After a night of rain;
The sun shone now as he rode
Past the long stone barn.
A Cockerel crowed
When he got down and strode,
Portly and bustling, to the farmhouse door,
Noisily knocking, noisily calling
"Fine day for a ride!
Anybody at home?" he cried.
No one replied.
He heard a muttered word,
The scrape of a chair on a flagstone floor.
A fumbled latch, and the door
Swung back. A man with lank black hair
Looked past him with unseeing stare.
Grey eyes he had, wild, bright
With a strange near-dazzling light
That faded as he recognised
His visitor: "From Porlock,
Sir?" he said, surprised,
"Come in", and moved his book and quill
From table-top to windowsill.
"His look was mazed, you'd say,
As if he were miles away",
A Porlock wife was told.
Miles away? How true!
He was away in Xanadu.

Harriet at Lynmouth, 1812

Honeymoon girl of seventeen,
She called it fairyland,
Their white cottage on a hillside,
Myrtles in its garden, roses
And honeysuckle on its walls.
Through her window the voice of the Lyn
And its bright waterfalls, its twin
Streams racing down a valley.
Leaning out, she thought of Shelley
Roaming the Valley of Rocks, drawing
Rock-shapes on old letters, putting
Political scribbles in bottles tossed in the sea
Or in toy balloons released in the summer sky.
His games made her laugh. His poetry puzzled her.
When he muttered
'How wonderful is Death,
Death and his brother Sleep!'
She said, 'Why think of Death?'
As they breathed the rose's breath,
And saw the honeysuckle twine
About their window-ledge,
Looking down at the sea's blue line
Hazily drawn round the harbour-edge,
He never thought of the Italian gulf,
Nor she of the cold Serpentine.

II: EXMOOR PLACES

'Exmoor Geometry' describes the shapes, both natural and man-made, that give the moorland landscape its special character. The thirty lines of 'Stone Circle' remembers a summer visit with three children (two of them probably Lawrence's own) to a ring of thirty stones. 'Exmoor Tale Teller' recalls legends of the moor and its earliest peoples. 'An Exmoor Thorn' and 'Exmoor Mistletoe' present vivid glimpses of Exmoor in late winter.

Exmoor Geometry

Arc of the moor's rim meets
The sky's circumference,
One segment of its area shaded black
By summer fires.
Irregular quadrilaterals of pasture
Pave the adjacent valley,
Brown parallelograms of ploughland,
And dark rectangles of woodland.
Cubes of cottages and barns,
White and grey and rusty red.
On the moorland ancient man has drawn
Stone circles and concentric rings,
Constructed elliptical barrows
And rough pyramids of cairns.
On the high ground his longstone drops
A stark perpendicular.

Stone Circle

Thirty stones in a ring,
Crouch under heavy weather,
Low little stones, lichen-veined,
Grey teeth stained with green;
Under a sky sullen with thunder,
Two boys and a girl, feet light on the heather,
Eyes intent on the map she carried.
"Stone Circle should be here!" one said.
"There!" she pointed, gazing ahead.
Then, in scorn, "Why, what a thing!
Stone Circle? More like a Fairy Ring!" she cried.
"What did they do inside, I wonder?
Dance? Pray? Make love?" Laughing,
The three joined hands, jumped into the ring,
Began to spin and twirl,
Ring a Ring O' Roses.
"Why, it's loose!" shrilled the girl,
One foot rocking a stone
To and fro in its socket.
Out came the bees, a dark smoke of bees,
Spiralling up from under the stone,
Wreathing black fumes around their heads,
Humming their rage for vengeance
So that the trio fled,
Slapping their arms, flapping their map,
Then started to laugh again,
But thinking now with dread
Of the underground place
Storing dark untouchable honey
Under the stone circle.

Exmoor Tale Teller

Eyes gleamed through fire-smoke,
Turned towards him while he spoke
To their circle squatted on his floor.
Flame flickered gold on his face
Scored like an oak's old bark.
Of these he told:
The giant stag whose antlers,
Picked up under ferns and branches,
A boy-dancer wore on their feast days;
The stag who drew his hunter after him
In a leap off the cliff-crag
For the sea to swallow;
The old chief asleep under the round cairn
On the clouded hillcrest, knees to chin,
And his ghost walking round it, keening
Under a white moon;
A girl sacrificed to the rain-god
Inside the stone circle
In the year of the drought
That cracked the skin of the moor;
Men ancient Tale Tellers talked of,
Men none had ever known,
Who killed a great bear
With stone axes they left on the moor.

An Exmoor Thorn

Ghost sheeted in white, the thorn tree
Startles the hind on her way to the pool
At dusk. Lambs have played all day
In the old brown bracken around it
While the unshorn ewes lay down
In its shade, and from the top branch,
Black shard on snow, a solitary crow
Watched with malignant eye.

Next month the hind will leave her calf
Among the bracken's green concealing croziers;
Green peggles will hang in clusters on the thorn,
Crimsoning daily as the year declines,
Until pigeons come with loud clapping wings,
To feast on a blood-red tree.

Wind from the sea runs shrieking
To snatch the yellow leaves,
Baring the thorn's spiked skeleton
That holds up a nest hanging sideways,
Untidy basket of black sticks.
In the bracken beneath grins the skull of a lamb,
Picked clean, bleached white,
Eye-sockets emptied.

Exmoor Mistletoe

Red sun setting, near its shortest day,
Over the heath throws a long red ray.
A man, jogging the track after foraging,
Sees it fall on a familiar knoll
Where the bent crab-tree grows,
Wizened, contorted, grey.
He has seen it like a pink cloud in spring,
Has plucked its bitter fruit,
Yet never before seen a green globe
Hanging under the branch
Where brown thrushes perch
And spatter droppings.

He cuts off the globe with his knife,
Turns it in horny hands, clucking with wonder
At the little green crescent leaves
And the berries like white bone beads,
Drops it into his deerskin pouch,
Trots on to his stone hut and woman,
Sets the green globe on a stone ledge
And tells her it is a magic plant
Growing in the strangest place
In winter, on a bare crab-tree branch.

III: EXMOOR PEOPLE

Several of Lawrence's poems celebrate the people who lived on Exmoor over centuries and millennia. The earliest, 'Nativity, Exmoor', imagines an unknown family living under the slopes of Dunkery Beacon at the time of Christ's birth. Dunkery appears again in 'Ladies in Snowdrop Valley', which retells the story of two refugee Huguenot sisters who died of privation in a rough shelter below the hill. 'Barbellion on Exmoor' recalls W.N.P. Barbellion, the penname of Bruce Cummings, son of a Barnstaple newspaper reporter. From childhood he had a passion for natural history, acquiring his knowledge through solitary study and dedicated observation. Poverty and illness frustrated his early ambitions. He obtained a post in the Natural History Museum, Kensington, but ill-health forced him to give up after a few years. A victim of multiple sclerosis (then untreatable) he recorded his life in his classic *The Journal of a Disappointed Man* (1919). Lawrence and her husband must have visited every church and graveyard on Exmoor. In 'Names of Exmoor Girls', she muses on the range of names given to local girls recorded over the centuries on stone, tablet and pages.

Nativity, Exmoor

Bright star ahead of him over Dunkery,
The only light tonight.
Moon is swallowed, lesser stars in flight
Beyond the scudding wrack of cloud.
The roof of the moor is black,
But this is the right way home.
Bare feet know the pattern of pebbles
Paving the track, the contours of moss,
The surface of slabs overlying a stream.
His eyes make out the tall stone
Standing in heather, his spine feels
Ripples of fear, and again when the magic thorn
Hooks his arm with a clawed finger.
The long mound lies beside the path,
Couched like a beast in the dark.

Now the path has topped the slope,
He sees the glow-worm light of home
And starts to trot as the track drops down.
A dead hare swings from his belt,
Taken in his withy-snare on the marsh.
His arrow has brought down a wild duck,
A handful of pebbles jingles in his pouch,
Gathered on the shore to please a woman.
His wattle hut dim with smoky reek,
Clay saucer of oil with glimmering wick,
An old woman babbling glad tidings
And his own woman on their bed of skins,
Holding, wrapped in lambskin,
A wailing, new-born child, streaked with blood.
Beyond unknown seas and mountains
Another child is born
Inside a stable,
Under a bright star.

Ladies in Snowdrop Valley

They walked here, I think, the two prim sisters,
Pale faces wrapped in Huguenot hoods,
One February day in their dreary exile,
Venturing down a rutted lane
Lured by the silver voice of the Avill,
Full of song after winter's rain,
Racing between woods
Of larch and birch, dancing
Over smooth stones, leaping
Mossed boulders and tossing foam
On the snowy sheets of flowers
Spread on the banks of the long green combe.
In tears, they remembered a glen
Deep in their harsh Cevennes
Where slim spears of snowdrops
Pierced the snow, and at night
Not deer but the wolf would roam.
From a shallow pool they gathered cresses,
Under a stone ledge found succulent snails,
And carried them back to their shack,
Under Dunkery Beacon,
Shut its door,
Turned its key.
Snow fell that night, relentlessly,
And they emerged no more.

Barbellion on Exmoor

Seventeen, already signed, so he said,
Into slavery, reporting court cases
In Barnstaple, illness and poverty
His oppressors. One day
He came to Challacombe,
Dropped in at the Ring O' Bells,
Talked with landlord and florid wife.
Thence he climbed steep Exmoor slopes
For the first time, turning his face
To a May Day breeze, saw a shepherd
With Exmoor sheep, and wrote
That his flood of delights was beyond recording.
Next year, after Petty Sessions in Lynton,
He discovered the Valley of the Rocks
And among 'those ribs of the earth'
Picked up a red viper, tied it with string
From a baker's cart and carried it home
On the Barnstaple train, home to his attic,
His microscope, his lonely zoology.

Exmoor, my El Dorado, he wrote,
Ten years after, listing first and last loves
When he lay near death,
Hoping to haunt those places.

Names of Exmoor Girls

On brown pages of registers,
On moss-crusted tombstones,
On wall-monument and flagstone,
In stained-glass windows
In Exmoor churches,
The names of girls
Gleaming like seashells
On a beach of brown stones.

Ilett and Avice,
Arminell, Wilmott,
Gelyan, Thomasin,
Where did they come from?
Some traveller's tale,
Or an old romance
From Flanders or France?
Susannah and Urith,
From a lost book of saints?
Alys and Izott,
From a troubadour's lay?
Who can say?
You find them today,
Among the Annes and Joans,
If you search,
In an Exmoor church.

IV: THE BRENDONS

The Brendons were one of Lawrence's favourite destinations. They were more accessible from her home than Exmoor, and more rugged than the Quantocks. In 'Naked Boy: Standing Stone' she celebrates a standing stone which is located just inside the National Park. Her haunting 'Deserted Village' commemorates the little hamlet of Clicket which was abandoned after the Brendons' phase of iron ore mining came to an end. 'At Leigh Barton' was written after she had attended an ecumenical service at a farm to mark the 350th anniversary of the death of Philip Powell (1594-1646). Powell, the son of Roger ap Rosser Powell and Catherine Morgan from Trallong in Wales, became Catholic chaplain to the Poyntz family at Leigh Barton, near Leighland, round about 1624 and was executed at Tyburn Hill in London on 30 June 1645. The fourth poem, 'Treborough Man', is more difficult to interpret. It appears to have been written after she visited the overgrown graveyard in Treborough. There is reference to Christian prayers, yet the funeral was pre-Christian. The link with the present-day flowers in the last two lines is typical of the ways in which she saw past and present as part of an unbroken chain.

Naked Boy: A Standing Stone

A winter's afternoon I came upon him,
Near the avenue of Brendon beeches
Naked as he, their creased old leaves discarded
And rustled by the wind. One way he looked
Through a field-gate at a flock of sheep,
Horned and black-faced, where he had seen the snipe
Drum up from the black bog, and labourers
Cutting long dykes and digging out the reeds.
To the left he saw the old hill-track
Curling through teazles and hemp agrimony.
He had seen it running free, had seen
The bronze-smith tramp it, carrying copper-cakes,
His casting-jets and bits of broken swords;
Watched a woman there, pulling meld by handfuls
(And, later, girls picking violets and berries),
Saw the wolf come loping where now the fox
Trots swift and agile, and the badger shuffles.

The roar, the swish of motor-traffic breaks
The silence of his long-accustomed place.
Stubborn he stands and watches as he watched
The horsemen and the waggons full of sheaves.
Soon they'll all be gone. He'll find himself
Alone as when he came. Less naked
Though. Grey lichen and green moss will wrap
A few more rags about his nakedness.

Deserted Village

Dead now, old people who remembered
Grandparents from Clicket.

Clicket too is dead, like a corner of Roman Gaul,
Buried in a valley cupped by Brendon Hills.
You can excavate it, find stones of a linhay-wall
Or a fragment of byre-pillar from a farm
Called Thorn or Combe;
Find a mill-stone cast under dead branches
Near the leat choked with many years' leaves,
Or a bit of leaded window from a cottage;
Discover Clicket among gorse-thickets and broom,
Among wilding fruit trees, Combe's orchard once,
Under rich layers of leaf-mould,
Beneath walnut-trees rifled by boys
Long after Clicket grew silent.

Silent, except for the notes of the stream
(They say there are trout there still),
Birdsong from a copse tangled with flowers,
Rustle of rabbit or stoat in bracken,
Bark of the fox after dark,
And moan of the wind through a roofless mill.

At Leigh Barton

Today they sang Vespers for him,
Choirboys from Downside Abbey, here
In this chapel redolent of hay,
Or so we think (men housed it here
Three centuries). Today
Catholic and Protestant kneel
Side by side, remembering his day
At Tyburn when he was made
'A spectacle for men and angels'.
Flowers in the chapel came
From Flowery Valley (Vallis Florida,
Named by monks of Cleeve).
Down that steep-dropping lane
He sometimes rode to visit friends
At Washford or Carhampton,
'Mr. Morgan from Leigh Barton',
Passing the wayside chapel of St. Pancras,
Its holy well, then Cleeve's old gatehouse,
Rosy in the sun.
In the woods the waterfall
Still tumbles loudly down a rocky face
To make a pool in which, they say,
He fished, and where, they say,
His ghost comes wandering.
Perhaps it paused today
Outside this chapel door
To hear the Abbey boys sing Vespers.

Treborough Man

The marker has gone, there is no trace
Of his resting-place
In the bleak churchyard of rustling grass
Where a few grey winter sheep have strayed
Where he was laid
By men in funeral black, who prayed
Their Christian prayers.
No monument, no epitaph,
He died before the cross had meaning,
Never knew our alphabet.

When others settled him to rest
Deep in the wood, in his stone chest,
What hymn was sung?
What prayer recited, in what tongue?
Maybe his spirit knows
This track he often trod
And walks it still, where the wind blows chill
And where the same plants grow
He used to know
Agrimony, alexanders, tormentil.

V: THE QUANTOCKS

Although the Quantock Hills were the focus for much research and prose writing by Lawrence and her husband, there were relatively few poems about them among her papers. Three of the four we've chosen have literary associations. 'Alfoxton' is about the home of William and Dorothy Wordsworth from 1797-98, the 'annus mirabilis' for English poetry. 'A Man At The Window' was written in 1972, the bicentenary of the birth of Samuel Taylor Coleridge, and refers to the small cottage, now called Coleridge Cottage, in Lime Street, Nether Stowey, where he wrote 'Frost at Midnight' in February, 1798. 'Bicknoller' recalls a description of the village scene by Richard Jefferies in his essay 'Summer in Somerset' (1888). The yew on the tower was removed some half century ago, but the tower and the yew are carved on one of the church's modern bench-ends (1932). Finally, 'Moorland Ponies' describes the herd that can still be seen on the verge of the Over Stowey to Crowcombe road across the Quantocks near Dead Woman's Ditch.

Alfoxton

The wizened beeches, bleached by salt winds,
Writhe on the ridge above the park.
High on the heath, in spring, the hawthorn-trees
Fly snowy flags over the sea of bracken.
Here the snorting ponies gallop,
Shaking their tangled manes.

Below, in Holford Glen –
They called it the Dell when
Wordsworth wrote his 'Lines in Early Spring' –
The birds still hop and play,
Primroses show their face,
Old fallen leaves lie heaped and crisp,
Rustling when an adder weaves its way.

The brook that Coleridge traced
Meanders its way to the sea,
Babbling the same light tune
That charmed his ear
And nearly made a poem.

A Man at the Window: A Sonnet for STC

Through this small window he had smelt the sweet
Summer breath of the lime-flowers, and the reek
Of nearby tan-pits; Wednesday every week
Had watched the carrier rumble up the street
To fetch his letters; children running by
Carrying the Quantock foxgloves in July,
Gipsies with whortleberries from the combes,
And broom-squires crying heather-headed brooms;
And carts for Christmas market with the store
Of holly from Alfoxden woods jolt past his door.
This February midnight Lime Street roofs shine bright
With diamond dust of frost and walls blanched white
By silent moon. Outside his window lies
The enchanter's world, the conjured paradise.

How the cold moonlight glitters in his eyes!

Bicknoller: In Memory of Richard Jefferies.

Still the old pathway throws a thin red band
Round green wheat fields on the sloping hill.
Above, a richer red, the new-ploughed land
Hangs cloak-like over the hill's green shoulder.
Gay and unsilenced still
The stream runs red
Over red stone and ruddy boulder,
Over twisted roots of oaks that stand
Splayfoot in the warm red earth ...
Vanished the mill ...
Split churchyard yew and lichened cross,
They stand here yet,
But higher now its head
Above the parapet,
The little yew a bird once set
Upon the church tower, red as faded rose.

Moorland Ponies

When the mad March wind is blowing
See them gallop down the track,
Long tails streaming, rough manes flowing,
In a wild excited pack.
See them lying in the heather
Sheltered from midsummer sun,
Drowsing on a bed of bracken
Till the daytime heat has gone.
Then you see them standing, drinking,
In the shallow reedy pool,
Making ripples and reflections
In the water clear and cool.
In winter-time they gather,
Against a ruined wall,
Huddled close together
As the snow begins to fall.

VI: SEDGEMOOR

Sedgemoor is part of the area now known as the Somerset Levels and Moors. Lawrence set the most successful of her two novels, *The Bond of Green Withy* (1954), on the flood-prone osier-growing beds of the Somerset Levels. She crossed the Levels by bus on weekdays when she was teaching at a convent at Langport. The three poems chosen here illustrate her use of legend and historical incidents to illuminate local landscapes. 'Sedgemoor Catalogue' has an intriguing note in brackets 'From a High Window' – perhaps alluding to Philip Larkin's *High Windows* (1974) – but provides no other clue to her viewpoint over the Levels. 'Night on Sedgemoor' recalls the defeat of the Duke of Monmouth's army at the Battle of Sedgemoor in Weston Zolyland in 1485. In 'Cadbury', Lawrence imaginatively reworks local traditions that South Cadbury was the location of Camelot.

Sedgemoor Catalogue (From a High Window)

Flat as your hand,
Broad land,
Green cloth stretched taut to Mendip's rampart,
Scattered with sheep like heaps of salt,
Strips of beige corn,
One burnt black
By a careless match,
Willows everywhere, silver in the wind,
Their roots in water, circling the pools,
Outlining the dykes.
In the middle, tiny Muchelney,
Brown stone, russet thatch.
Here sleep the bones of monks
Who in time of flood
Took boats over this land
To cut their reeds
And catch their eels.

Night on Sedgemoor

Out of white mist the crooked willows
Lift their polled heads.
On the long dyke, a water-fowl
Moves in the reeds.
The soft-feathered owl goes flighting over
Cattle bowed down to graze the clover,
Utters her cry, prolonged and eerie,
Utters her age-old mournful query:
"Who lies here? Who? Who?"
Under the earth and grass and rushes,
Dust has stirred.
Under a lagging moon, the night-wind
Carries their word.
"We who sleep here be Monmouth's men
Dreaming we drive the plough again,
Fodder our beasts and cut the peat
For our Sedgemoor hearths. How sweet
Could the dream come true!"

Cadbury

Some say that Camelot stood here
On the hill-top fort inside these four great rings.
Here came Arthur, noblest of kings,
Mordred and Bedwyr and Guinevere.
Some have heard them late on Christmas Eve,
King and knights with bridles jingling,
Riding down the rough hill-way to the spring
At Sutton Montis. Here
By the crooked Cam he got his death-wound.
They carried him, great Arthur on his bier,
Down to the causeway in the marsh –
Lost now beneath the ground
Of Cadbury fields – and all the way
To Glastonbury and the melancholy mere.
Now cattle graze inside these rings,
Trample bluebells on the wooded slopes,
Their bull standing sullen on the stony path.
Day after day the fighter planes
Diving and turning, scream defiance
Over Camlann, Arthur's final field,
And Camelot's empty hall.

VII: MELANCHOLY

For the most part Lawrence's poems are optimistic. But in a few there is a strain of sadness. Some are about minor regrets. Typical of these is 'The Old Pond', in which a loved field pond is filled in and the boys no longer slide on the ice. In 'Meadow Close' she regrets the building of houses behind her own garden and the sheep who once grazed it. But there is a darker side. In contrast to her many joyful poems about Christmas is her 'Christmas Child', in which a small boy witnesses the horror of King Herod's purge of all male children under two. 'Haworth Postman' appears to be about the disappointment of one of the Bronte sisters. Finally, in 'The Wind and the Dark' Lawrence hints at the coming darkness at the end of life.

The Old Pond

Where the grass is darker,
In the middle of the field,
There lay the old pond,
A crooked willow beside it
And a clump of reeds
Where the moorhen nested.

In sunlight it shone like silver,
On cloudy days it lay leaden,
On rainy nights a mist trailed over it,
Curdled and white as milk.

Huge carthorses galloped into it,
Released from plough and wagon,
Took long gulping drinks
And swished their heavy manes.
In summer cattle stood cooling,
Eyes half-shut, tails whisking flies.
In winter boys slid on the ice,
Shouting with out-flung arms.
When the moon was full its image lay
Upon the pond like a round yellow cheese
And drunken revellers, so they say,
Tried to fish it out and carry it home.

The farmer filled in the pond;
His cattle and horse drink from a trough;
Our revels are ended.

Meadow Close

Today they put sheep in the field behind my house.
It was a real field once
Before they built a hundred houses nearby.
An estate named Meadow Close.
So that the field became a 'green space'
Where boys kick a ball and the summer fete
Is held.
But today there are sheep in there,
Black faces in winter fleeces
With a blue initial on every back.
They bunched themselves at first into a grey rosette
In the middle of the ground, bewildered,
Afraid to move.
Then took courage and fanned out
In two nearly-straight lines,
And dropped down their heads to feed.
Standing at the fence, I hear the sound of their teeth
Biting the grass,
And the sound makes the place a real field again.
I would not be surprised
If the fence of post and wire
Turned into a quickset hedge
Ready to spike tufts of wool on its thorns.

A Christmas Child

In the winter night
A two-year boy,
His mother's pride and joy
Woke and saw a ray of light
From a lantern fall
Through the slit in the wall,
Heard the tap of crooks
On the stony street,
And the shambling tread
Of eager feet.
Days later, his mother cried
"Look!", dropped her distaff
And carried him outside
To watch three camels as they strode
Morosely past, their heads a-sway.
Black-bearded, purple-cloaked, the men who rode
And asked a passer-by the way.
Days later, as he plays
With shells on the floor
He stares at a man
Who darkens the door.
Laughs when the helmet catches the light
As the man moves his head,
Laughs at the great sword in his hand
Glittering bright:
The sword is red.

Haworth Postman

A brown dot in the sea of grasses,
She stands peering through her glasses
At something that moves invisible,
Not the postman, only a sheep
That has strayed from the flock;
Something moves near the grey rock –
Only a cloud-shadow's sweep.
Now, at last, a man with a pack,
Trudging along the farmhouse track
On slow deliberate feet;
She feels her heart beat,
A letter! Yet what does he say?
'Nowt for Parsonage today.'
Nothing has come, no, not a crumb
Of comfort, not even a word.
Behind her glasses
Her eyes are blurred,
They see a foreign street
While grasses rustle
Around her feet.

The Wind and the Dark

Outside my window tonight
The wind and the dark keep company,
Shapeless and dense,
Pressing on the panes.
No ray of moonlight, no star,
Not the greatest planet,
Shines through,
And the huge constellations are lost.
The wind talks,
Sometimes in sibylline whispers,
Then in a low-throated roar,
Tells of ocean and continent,
Mountain, valley, meadows and flowers,
Of cities and their towers,
Then murmurs 'Sleep'.
When you wake, I'll be gone.
So will the dark.
Enjoy the sun while you may.
We'll return, one night, me and the dark,
To call on you,
And the dark will hold you for ever.
Vanished the sun and the moon,
The stars and constellations.

VIII: MEMORIES

In most of her writing, both poetry and prose, Lawrence keeps a distance from her personal life. But some poems appear to relate to her personal experience and memories. The earliest example is in 'Moon Daisies' where she recalls walking as a four-year old with her mother across a Buckinghamshire field, probably on their own farm. In 'Boulevard Fleuri' she recalls her undergraduate days when she was only twenty, studying in France as part of her university course. In 'Nightingales of the Auvergne' there is her trademark broad sweep of time from Roman Gaul to Nazi Vichy. But the references to 'two lovers' may refer to her and Jack, both then in their early twenties, first meeting in this lovely part of rural France. In 'Pebble from a Barrow' she is walking on Exmoor with her son, Christopher. In 'Man in the Moon' yet another generation has passed as she recalls watching a moon landing on TV with her grandson, while thinking back to her own grandfather telling her stories of the 'man in the moon'. In 'Charles's Wain' Lawrence looks up at the constellation usually called the Plough but is also known as Dick and his Waggon.

Moon Daisies: A Sonnet

One of my memories, older than any other:
A four-year child, walking with my mother,
In a June meadow ready for mowing,
Tall grasses around us, green ocean far-flowing
As the breeze flitted over it, blowing
Cloud-shadows. In afternoon light
The green sea extended beyond my sight.
Drawn on its surface, strokes of white
Made lines of foam, trembling and swaying,
Moon-daisies in hundreds, nodding, playing
With the breezes, rippling and bending,
Drawing white lines that looked never-ending,
A golden eye shone when a flower turned its head
"They're called marguerites", my mother said.

Boulevard Fleuri

Boulevard Fleuri they called it,
A street in a grey French town.
Why did they name it so?
The only flowers I saw there
Were petunias wilting in a window box.
Was its paving laid over a strip of meadow
Coloured by cowslips, lady smocks,
Buttercups and daisies?
Perhaps that's the reason for its name.
I was twenty when I walked that boulevard,
And my feet trod, not on paving-stones,
But on young grass and wild flowers.

Nightingales of the Auvergne

You have travelled the thousand miles of skyway
To this valley in the mountains of the Auvergne
Under the old dead volcanoes.
From each bush, from each ledge in the rocks,
Jets your song of delight and passion.
In the villa-gardens, every lilac tree
Pours forth that song with its fragrance.
One villa was the Nazi Centre of Interrogation,
Your song the last sound some of its inmates heard.
The men of Gaul heard you singing
As they trudged to the plateau Gergovia
To meet the Roman invaders.

Tonight, two lovers stand in the moonlight
Hand in hand, believing you sing
For them alone.

Pebble from a Barrow

The child ran ahead
Along the track through the spread acres
Of heather, winter-black,
Climbed nimbly and stood alone
On the Bronze Age mound;
Ran back to press something into my hand.
"Look what a pretty stone I found!" –
A piece of yellow quartz thrown
On top of the cairn. I had known
Always that somebody crouched beneath,
Had thought of him as a skeleton,
A collection of bones, without breath.

Suddenly I knew him a man,
Familiar like me with the water-scarred track
And the sombre heathland, whose child ran
Ahead of him picking up stones
And ran swiftly back
To thrust a pebble into his hand,
A coloured one,
This stone that was warm
From the clasp of my son.

No, it was the warmth of his hand mine knew
As I shivered in the wild
Exmoor wind, and clasped the yellow stone
Picked up by a child
On the roof of his chambered skeleton.

Man in the Moon

When I was five
My grandfather showed me
The Man in the Moon.
He lived in a cave
In the mountains of the moon.
The cave was full of silver.
He lived there with his dog.
I saw them plainly
When I stared at the huge full moon.

Tonight, on a flickering screen,
I showed my grandson
The man on the moon,
Booted and goggled,
Kicking up moon dust
Picking up moon rock.
"Look! He has a little cart",
Cried the child, delighted.

Charles's Wain

Grandfather showed me Charles's Wain,
High in the sky tonight,
A starry waggon of golden grain
On wheels of glittering light;

Grandfather showed me Charles's Wain,
Drawn by its golden team,
A waggon that travelled a starry lane
By the side of a starry stream.

IX: THE FOUR SEASONS

Seasons are a recurring theme in Berta's poems for children. She clearly wished to share her own love of the constant turning of the year around her Somerset home. There were many poems to choose from so selection was not easy. After an opening poem called 'Seasons' we chose three short poems to illustrate each of the four seasons. For spring these are 'Yellow Spring', 'April Garden' and 'Swallows'; for summer, 'June Scents', 'Midsummer' and 'Lazy Summer'; for autumn, 'Summer's End', 'Apples' and 'Red Feast'; and for winter, 'Jack Frost', 'Season of Sleep' and 'Blackthorn Winter'.

Seasons

Spring smells of growing grass,
Of buds and showers;
Summer smells of new-mown hay
And open flowers;
Autumn smells of woodman's fires
And garnered grain;
Winter smells of fallen leaves
Drenched with rain,
Of frosty soil turned by the plough,
And snow piled white on roof and bough.

Yellow Spring

It is a yellow spring:
Jessamine falls
Over the garden fence,
Forsythia kindles a blaze
Under its walls,
And the last riband of daffodils
Trails through the growing grass.
At night in a sky pricked with stars,
The comet swims,
Yellow fish with glittering tail,
Till the stars grow pale
And waking birds see it drown
In the yellow light of the sun.

April Garden

It is a painted garden
Behind the window-glass,
Tulips upright as Roman centurions
Red-helmeted,
Daffodils lissom as dancing-girls,
Saffron-skirted,
Polyanthus in page-boy velvet,
Crimson and maroon, buttoned with gold.
Grass and leaves
Vivid viridian.

Swallows

Hark to the shrilling of swallows,
Swooping above my head,
Leaving the pools and meadows,
The nests in the old thatched shed.

Tales they are telling, the swallows,
Of a faraway, sun-lit home,
Far-off countries, foreign cities,
France, and Athens, and Rome.

They sing of lonely islands
Set in a sapphire sea,
Of mountains, valleys and rivers,
Names unknown to me.

Others will see them in the spring,
Gathering overhead,
Singing of pool and meadow,
Orchard and old thatched shed.

June Scents

The morning breeze
That ruffles the trees,
Brings scent of the hay
Made yesterday.

Mid-afternoon,
And the golden heat,
Draws scent from the rose,
Haunting and sweet.

When evening brings
A shower of rain,
Wild honeysuckle
Scents the lane.

Gardens are dark,
No star in sight,
And scent of the lilies
Embalms the night.

Midsummer

Today is the sun's great festival,
Today he is riding high,
The wheels of his chariot flashing fire
As he travels across the sky.

The sun's own children, marigolds
And sunflowers with golden rays,
Stand in bloom near the garden path,
Setting the border ablaze.

Roses and peonies open wide,
Hanging their heads full-blown,
The scent of summer wafts from the hay
Lying in fields new-mown.

Birds are silent in noonday heat,
Not a leaf stirs on the trees,
The only sound - near the lavender hedge –
The humming of bees.

Lazy Summer

Idly the days of summer pass,
Lazy the shadows on the grass,
Lazy the clouds that sail on high
Like galleons in the summer sky.

In the heat of summer noon,
Softly the sleepy pigeons croon.
Lazily now the roses shed
Their silken petals, white and red.

Butterflies drowse through noonday hours,
Half asleep on summer flowers.
Bees that into larkspurs creep
Drone and hum as if half-asleep.

Summer's End

Her last silken petals
The rose has shed,
Now the last swallow
Southbound has fled.

Thistledown gossamer
Floats on the breeze,
Apples blush crimson
On the old apple trees.

Where the bright cornfield
Stood in the sun,
Stretches the stubble,
Harvest is done.

Later each morning
The sun throws his ray;
Heavy the dew,
At the end of the day.

Apples

They hang in hundreds
On the stooping tree,
Scarlet-streaked, golden-skinned,
Turgid with juice,
Globes glowing in October's sun,
So they hung,
Over naked Eve in Eden
When she stretched her hand to pluck forbidden fruit
Round and perfect as her breasts,
While the serpent, twined about the trunk,
Watched her with a jewelled eye,
Persuaded her with honeyed tongue.
So they hung
Over the head of Guinevere
Riding to destruction
Through valley-orchards of Avalon.
An old man will pick them tomorrow,
Creaking like an old bough on his ladder,
Pick them with hands engrained with earth
And stained with tobacco,
But gentle on satin skin of apples.

Red Feast

Outside my window,
In three gardens on my street,
The feast is spread,
Crimson, scarlet and red, blood-red,
A berry feast, a merry feast
For voracious starlings, thrushes
Plump with apple-eating,
Saucy blue tits,
They come crowding,
A noisy meeting,
To cotoneaster, haws, blood-red holly,
Still they come, as mist starts shrouding
Steeple, cottages, fields and street,
Before the fall of night
And fall of sleet.

Will those others come,
Who came ten years ago,
When the great snowfall followed the frost?
That multitude of waxwings, lost
On their flight from the north,
When the red feast called them forth
Out of the lowering sky,
So the street was loud
With a flickering, twittering crowd,
Fluttering red-waxed wings
On snowy boughs laden with winter berries
Red as summer cherries.

Jack Frost

Silver Pencil in hand,
Jack Frost came here,
On windowpanes throughout the land,
Drew pictures clear.

Slippered soft in furry white
Over fields he crept,
To sketch on windows in the night,
While children slept.

In silver tints his pictures grew
Through long night hours;
White shells, white ferns, white leaves, he drew,
And shining flowers.

Season of Sleep

It's a time to sleep
When winter falls;
Butterflies creep
Into cracks of walls.

The humble bee
For weeks will dwell
Asleep in the dark
Of his bank side cell.

In a hollow tree
All night, all day,
The dormouse drowses
The hours away.

Lost in sleep
The hedgehog lies curled
In a ditch of brown leaves,
His secret world.

Blackthorn Winter

Second winter is here
Colder than the first
Although iris and crocus
Have burst from prison
And light cuts cloud with a steel blade
Later every afternoon;
A ribbon of old snow
Trails along a hedge-bank,
Wind blows dry as metal
Through a gap in the hedge
Where a fox stands, drooping his brush,
Eying innocent lambs
In a glistening field.
When snow loaded the hedge to breaking-point
Winter was kinder;
Now blackthorn piles weightless drifts upon it
Winter is bitter.

X: NATURE, FIELDS AND FLOWERS

This is a group of poems, largely directed at children, which celebrates country fields and wayside flowers. 'Field Map', like 'Exmoor Geometry', draws attention to the landscape's various shapes while 'The Green Wheatfield' ponders on changes to come as the crop grows and ripens. 'The Old Paddock' shows the diversity of field flowers and evokes childhood memories of a much-loved pony. Of Lawrence's many 'flower' poems we select three. 'Daffodils' follows her favourite theme of imagining old scenes from a present scene. 'Roadside Garden', was her last poem, written on her 97th birthday.

Field Map

Beyond this window
The flat fields lie
Like a map unrolled
Beneath the sky.

Here is a field
Where on April days
Buttercups kindle
A golden blaze.

Here is a field
Called Shepherd's Mead
Where off-white sheep
Peacefully feed.

Here is a field
That the plough stripes brown
As the red tractor
Moves up and down.

In the farthest field
A silvery gleam
Is the winding course
Of a tiny stream.

The Green Wheatfield

Soon the tall green wheat will stand
Where we saw the ploughed brown land;
Blades of green have forced their way
Upward to the light of day.

Clouds will let their shadows glide
Across the field, from side to side;
Summer breezes, passing by,
Make the wheat ears sway and sigh.

Here the lark will drop to rest,
Here her fledglings safely nest,
Here the tiny harvest mouse
Will frisk and climb and make her house.

Here the blue cornflower will grow,
Here the scarlet poppies blow;
Here will nod the marguerite,
In among the tall green wheat.

The Old Paddock

Behind, the farmhouse, ruined now,
The empty paddock lies.
Rough teazles barricade the gate,
Alive with butterflies.

Blackberries load the straggling hedge
Of this forgotten place,
Under them wild violets grow,
Arum and Queen Anne's lace.

In the tall grass a skylark nests,
Woodpeckers drill a tree,
The rabbits frolic unafraid,
The badger shuffles, free.

Long years ago at morning light,
The farmhouse children came,
To find their pony grazing here,
And called him by his name.

Old Lane

Down a lonely lane
We children knew
In a marshy nook
The kingcups grew.

Dog-roses bloomed
High in the hedge,
Foxgloves stood sentry
Along its edge.

At the foot of an elm
In March we found
White violets clustered
Close to the ground.

Near the cornfield stile
We children knew,
Scarlet and proud
The poppies blew.

Daffodils

Shakespeare saw them
Peering through the grass of Stratford meadows
Before the first swallow skimmed the Avon.
Milton saw them
Lifting cups of gold filled with dewy tears
To strew upon his dead friend's hearse.
Herrick saw them
Dancing all day in his Devon orchard
Fading by the time of Evensong.
Wordsworth saw them
Dancing, fluttering, tossing their heads
By the sparkling waves of Ullswater.

Four Winds

North wind, rough wind,
Roaring through the trees,
Bringing snow to mountains,
Tempest to the seas.

South wind, soft wind,
Breathing scent of flowers,
Waking sleeping butterflies,
To dance through sunny hours.

East wind, spiteful wind,
Whistling down the street,
Parching every ploughland,
Strewing fields with sleet.

West wind, sweet wind,
Bringing gentle rain,
Making summer meadows
Fresh and green again.

Wild Geese

A trumpet-call
In the northern sky!
From their Arctic home
The wild geese fly.

Great wings beating,
Formation plain,
Wild geese making
An outstretched skein.

From a lone white world
The wild geese fly,
Over icefield and mountain,
Miles through the sky.

Far overhead
The wild geese pass,
Searching and seeking
Fields of green grass.

Reflections

Sometimes at evening I have seen
The meadow streamlet shining green,
And two great swans as white as snow
Swimming in the sunset glow.

Among the sedge and iris shoots,
Among the willows' tangled roots,
There the rosy cloudlets lie,
Fallen from the sunset sky.

Near the stream, as clear as glass,
There I wait and watch them pass,
Four great swans, as white as snow,
Two on the water, two below.

Roadside Garden

This rambling roadside pathway
Its own small garden grows.
Here bloom the trailing bindweed
And the fair white rose.

Cow parsley, ragged robin,
Grow on hedgerow banks,
And higher up the foxgloves
Parade in gorgeous ranks.

Primroses, like a starburst,
Cover the lower side,
And in its smallest crannies
The white wild violets hide.

Acknowledgements

The title *Stepping Westward* is taken from Wordsworth's poem of the same name composed during his tour of Scotland in 1803 with his sister and Coleridge. It reflects Lawrence's westward move in 1932 from her native Buckinghamshire and her adopted France to Somerset, where most of her poems were written and where she sometimes stepped, literally and metaphorically, in Wordsworth's, Dorothy's and Coleridge's footsteps.

The following poems were first published in the *Exmoor Review*:
'At Ash Farm', 'At Leigh Barton', 'Barbellion on Exmoor', 'Culbone', 'Deserted Village', 'Exit from Cleeve', 'Exmoor Geometry', 'Exmoor Mistletoe', 'Exmoor Tale Teller', 'An Exmoor Thorn', 'Harriet at Lynmouth, 1812', 'Ladies in Snowdrop Valley', 'A Man at the Window', 'Naked Boy', 'Names of Exmoor Girls', 'Nativity, Exmoor', 'Pebble From a Barrow', 'Stone Circle', and 'Treborough Man'.

The following poems were first published in *Children's Education*:
'Charles's Wain', 'The Fields of Barley', 'Jack Frost' and 'Reflections'.

In editing the verse, this book draws on the original version of each poem as collected by Christopher Lawrence from his mother's papers (and reproduced in *A Somerset Voice*) rather than in any previously published version.

The colophon on the front cover is taken from a linocut by Berta's husband, Jack Lawrence and appears in her *Quantock Country* (Westaway Books, 1952). It shows part of a carved bench-end in the parish church of Crowcombe lying on the western lee of the Quantock Hills. It was probably carved by a Somerset craftsman, Simon Warman, around 1534.

We are grateful to Adrian Lewis for permission to use his wonderful photograph "Megalith 2, Stanton Drew" on our cover.

❖

Peter Haggett (on behalf of the original three who collected Berta's work) and Suzie West nee Lawrence (on behalf of Berta's family), wish to record their thanks to Tom Furniss for expertly editing these poems. We hope in published form they will allow Berta's distinctive verses to be widely enjoyed by all those who love the English landscape.

The late Dr Chris Lawrence, Berta Lawrence's son, was a burns specialist at the Birmingham Queen Elizabeth Hospital.

The late John Allen was formerly Regional Director of the British Council.

Peter Haggett, Emeritus Professor of Geography, Bristol University, is the author or editor of over 30 books on geographical practice, theory and individual research topics. He has held numerous teaching posts and visiting professorships around the world and was awarded a CBE in 1993, for 'services to urban and regional geography'.

Tom Furniss taught English Literature at the University of Strathclyde for thirty years. His books include *A Kind of Making: Selected Poems, 1979-2018* (Coverstory Books, 2019), *Triple Measures: New Poems by K.M. Miller, Ian Gouge and Tom Furniss* (Coverstory Books, 2020), and (with Michael Bath) *Reading Poetry: An Introduction* (Routledge, 1996, 2007).

www.ingramcontent.com/pod-product-compliance
Lightning Source LLC
Chambersburg PA
CBHW021117080526
44587CB00010B/554